EPIGRAMS

T0329445

Bill F. Ndi

Langaa Research & Publishing CIG
Mankon, Bamenda

Publisher:
Langaa RPCIG
Langaa Research & Publishing Common Initiative Group
P.O. Box 902 Mankon
Bamenda
North West Region
Cameroon
Langaagrp@gmail.com
www.langaa-rpcig.net

Distributed in and outside N. America by African Books Collective
orders@africanbookscollective.com
www.africanbookcollective.com

ISBN: 9956-727-97-0

DISCLAIMER
All views expressed in this publication are those of the author and do
not necessarily reflect the views of Langaa RPCIG.

Table of Content

Foreword

Through light and darkness that colour human imagination and warrant the birth of poetry, will the reader find peace of mind, laughter, hilarity, mirth and elation in the everyday simple words in this painful journey through which the author takes one. Epigrams are daily reflections on most human foibles with useful hints on how to go about these issues of life which most would think impenetrable; and would like to avoid all their entrapments. Like a torch bearer lighting the foggy path of the inner labyrinth, these epigrams will take the reader through the impervious and winding perception of things human, illuminating the path all humans should tread on.

Acknowledgement

Here, the poet would like to acknowledge the very useful contribution of those who in one way or the other helped to make the realization of this collection possible. I would start by making it clear that (which is a platitude) being a poet in the 21st century is an uphill task both ways. So, I would like to seize this opportunity to thank most especially my *friend-brother* and wife, Festus and Eugenia Frundeh who have not only been my benefactors but showed understanding of the plight of the 21st century poet mentioned above and as a result armed me with the necessary logistic support needed to have a level head for reflection and writing.

I would also like to heartily thank my colleagues at Tuskegee University for their support and most especially, Dr. Fishkin for writing the preface to this collection.

Again, Professor Emmanuel Fru Doh of Century College Minnesota must also be acknowledged here for meticulously going through this collection in its manuscript form and making useful suggestions, pointing out the typos that would have blurred the clarity and lucidity of these epigrams.

Over and above, how can I forget my little nephew Mark Che Frundeh who would always remind me every evening before he goes to bed, "Uncle Bill, go and work on your computer; right!"

Finally it would be hard for me to end without extending a word of recognition to the publisher and editors who warrant this to be available to a larger public.

It is difficult to list everyone, but to all of you who have me in your positive prayers, THANK YOU!

Preface

Bill F. Ndi's epigrams cover a wide range of topics. The notion that Freedom is "celestial" is catching (3). Their most striking features are criticisms of human behaviour. This happens quite a bit with the "sausage making" side humans as, perhaps, the most powerfully disturbing image (95).

These epigrams often come with the imagery of the human heart. All of which bring to mind, John Donne, especially with the pun on "wholly" and "Holy" (90). Also they feature frequent commentary on love in all its forms with a strong emphasis on feelings and emotions. More than once, the psyche is the focus. The references to "inner life" and "inner peace" are particularly arresting.

The theme of inner quiet is very powerful in the "Epilogue to Epigrams". What comes to mind is that the world is a very inhospitable place. The notion is that the world, especially cities, is angry and unwelcoming. Often, the political examination is spun on illuminating pessimism – perhaps this is unavoidable. Epigram 48 is my favorite.

Benjamin H. Fishkin
Dept. of English & Foreign languages
Tuskegee University, Alabama, USA.

Preface to Epigrams

There is nothing epigrammatic
About epigrams
Just as there is nothing liveable
About life
'Cause as Landlord of a cavern
nothing earthly is thine plight.
So epigrams per se
Are doggerels
With their ragged and silly comedy.

(1)

If one told thee
In love there was 'rithmetic,
With one word, retort:
LIE!
Supply
Her with emotion
If she seeks thine opinion
'Cause She springs from the Heart
never from the head!

(2)

Nice guy
Show thy love to any
And as they back reciprocity
Welcome another....
But if all negate,
Show them, hitchless is
Life without them
And if any, imagination
In the self will defy that!

(3)

freedom like the Almighty
a very expensive commodity
whose price cannot be got
like that of pot
is celestial
not artificial
planted in the hearts
beyond the heads
flying birdlike in the sky!

(4)

In city
Sagacity
The know-nothing
Know everything
Is wisdom
In quackdom;
A knife
For the naïve;
Stools for seating this sole
Grave memoir to poor souls
Drowning riches
For natural itches!

(5)

Everyone is scared of Black,
That in which I find the Universe
As it drops on white, all say: "stain!"

This attention-attraction injects thoughts
Of the cool calm night, evil,
With one thing ununderstood:
How white petals clustered
On dark green leaves
Are discarded stain;
Ha! Ha! Ha!

(6)

The Soldier's load
Is one big
Load
Blindfolding the Masses
Turning down
Mamman Jiya's[1] "Song for
A Bird
That Sings
For Rain."

---

[1] One of the few brains ever to have served in the military. Nigerian General and world class poet!

(7)

When the inner man is small
Nowhere but from arithmetic platform,
On which one and one
Give two, does all gleam;
Far from truism
'Cause for creators
'Tis union or more,
making, in the manner of the Hellenes
the lonesome think and laugh…!

(8)

Jokes must be loathed!
Thought the bray matter skull,
Shielding practicality
Objectifies Man; not until
He digs out of jokes, fun,
And rattles
The ribs,
The lungs,
For these !

(9)

The stars of the sky
Reflect man's nature
And anyone hitching another
Plays none but a humble role,
A passer's-by;
The star to shine bleak or bright
Does so without clouds
Though with them the bright
Could be blurred a while…!

(10)

As a laughing man
Cries at heart
So does the crier laugh at heart
For any sapien
Would not on another's toe
Crack jokes to see his
Lachrymal stream flow;
Flowing from the heart or source.
The oneness of happiness is the greatest!

(11)

Sundays' services
All is eschatology!
Yet, the litany
Is punctuated with:
"World without end!"
For everybody
To nod
"Amen."
Irony…?

(12)

Thinking someone mad
Is in itself, madness;
'Cause you need meet one of them
Chat with 'm
And discover he with the heart sees;
The faculty you lack!
Having that you lack
Should higher their stand
Even when they live on sand!

(13)

Determining men
From their past, macadamises pavement
To abhorrent larynx vibration.
One is not even what one does
Or says of oneself,
Nor what others think and say of one;
But, one is one's inner self:
As a repented thief or rapist is any neither;
Or one is, only from within, either!

(14)

Any man who leaves
Himself at women's mercy
Is weak but not as an intellectual
With emotions as rituals;
So confused....
That his import goes
Not to cranial content
But, years put for certification
Singing certification education!

(15)

As we keep pace with our shadows,
We are alive and faster than it,
We head towards catastrophe,
And slower than he,
Drawing near God's acre.
Development's pace in our worlds
Must be ours
Else we'll be seeking
Acridity and the Sea King

(16)

Project yourself everything,
Reject nothing
Of equal opportunity shoes;
Thinking yourself something
In these shoes
Without
Doubt
In you will you see
Real nothing!

(17)

Meeting
A being, known
Or unknown
Generates nothing
But an opportunity
For partisans to credit
Or discredit
Specifically, Humanity,
And Nature at large!

(18)

The poet's gift
Is a drift
To spot stain
And strain
A Saint;
Paint
Beauty
From the ugly
With figures!

(19)

Black tragedy,
Farce story
Of teaching
A child walking
And before she creeps,
She is said free;
Senseless vain multi-coloured cloth on tree
Whizzing dependence hail Real Ovation
To chant independence in Prizin the "Nation."

(20)

Before you live
And leave
Taste of the Genesis
Of dogs' and cats'
Enmity who's
Language norm
Born
For one, a wag is friendship,
For the other, war, it depicts!

(21)

Gloom flashes beams
When the cosmos gleams
Bleak with dearth knocking at doors
For prostitute love to sneak in through   windows
Leaving humour alone
To retort foundation,
Supporting roots
To stabilising
The set crumbling…!

(22)

Fans' goal is whirlwind's
Speeding more than he;
Yet, her discomfort's proportion leadens fan's
Comfort's, she eggs world deem her repute;
Blurring docility
Parent of respectability
Like life's major irony:
Squeezing water out of stone!
But rocks are springs' sources…!

(23)

Not writing nor
Open confrontation
Arms against oppression
Triumph; though freeing the psyche
Through these media at bay
Keep one till one fateful day
Hands him an invitation
To lie sleepily still
In its solitary creel.

(24)

Men think IDEAL
Stimulates quest if 'tis real?
Horizon bleak, viewing it
Mount great messy sh…t
Like a cult leader,
His clayey feet a lure
Baits them; his followers
Promising heaven
And Drawing them Hell Bound…!

(25)

We laugh in life
And at times at life
'Coz of ignorance
hurtling arrogance
screening
'n shielding
Laughter,
Mystery's mother
Take us uphill…!

(26)

… Knew no difficulty
Felt Liberty
In this inhumane
Human world…
…………………………………………
…………………………………………
…………………………………………
…………………………………………
Anymore word …!

(27)

Friendship
Determined by flock of sheep
From humanity steals
His lonely assets,
Honesty,
Degenerating 'm senseless;
Of its genetic gift
Deprives him it
Clothing 'm manly…!

(28)

At a point in every man's span
He his hand dipped in a pan;
Looking back at his decision
Made him, all his life, Little Malcolm.
The action's goal, not to hurt!
The results hurt;
From misreading,
Egged on by impulsion
We need seek its burial…!

(29)

Thinking silence
Conformity
Borders upon stupidity
For lightning's presence
Signals thunderous bolt
With nefarious darkness
In which when lit up
You hardly can sup;
And all you can is crawl…!

(30)

Life's essence
Is to quest joy,
Envisaging happiness;
That of others,
And whether happiness can be
When others are moody?
Castigate nothing of a brother
Seek what's liveable
About his being and in him…!

(31)

Tears I see streaming
Down
When you see them flowing
Down a woman's cheeks
How genuine…!
Ha!
Ha!
Ha!
Genuine …! Tears…. Genuine?

August, 15th 1993.

(32)

What's being alive?
To be alive is not to live.
To be alive is to have a conscience,
Feel for others
When you inconvenience
Them; without hesitation
Ask for pardon!
To be alive is having others' mind
As you move about, in mind…!

June, 11th 1995.

(33)

Just as all other
Human Inventions die
So shall racism
The worst of the isms
That has so decimated
The heartless man.

After having in their rave
Harboured ideas not so grave,
Those thinking black power
Shall find weakness in death
And so shall those thinking white supremacy
Have their illusions
Shattered in their grave
The one, off-spring to
the mother.

(34)

in life
were everything
freedom
crowned
then anarchy
would reign supreme
and supremely
will freedom
be drowned...!

(35)

When you reciprocate love
Loving truly for even just one minute
None would ever mind
Asking you if you harboured thoughts
At all; the love would forever last
And all shall forever
Love, care
And cherish you
The winner…!

13/01/2004.

(36)

We've all had that beautiful dream
The dream of that wonderful piece of cake
We would either want to eat

And have

Or have

And eat without ever exhausting

And life replicates it:
Too bad, life has a beginning!
So shall it come to an end!

(37)

One third of the efforts and energies put into wars would have turned the world a better place; one without misery: diseases, poverty, illiteracy, etc. The Royal Court in which Fraternal Love and Solidarity and Happiness reign as Masters…. were they in this direction used! Now, let's keep on dreaming till one day at polls, we purge our World of the power hungry who see nothing of the hungry majority and would brandish our personal security for guise of going to introduce elsewhere the brothel in which chaos is the Mistress; that which we abhor!

What a waste!

(38)

"*My* child is bad!" Exclaimed a parent.
 A child near-by hearing this, turned and said:
"through the path of wisdom, lead that gift of continuity allowing him space for childish pranks for no child is completely bad!
Not until he turns out to adulthood   useless
                    and
      hopeless,
then you may think your cause lost!
But then, all liability at their own cost!"
Hope for, pray for, and dream of a reformation even in the hereafter....

(39)

Still the masses
Duck-tape their mouths
Mobilise your might to immobilise all
But, let the trees
Rattle their leaves
As the wind passes
For the masses
To enjoy the music
From that current transporting
And changing
The Geography of politics

(40)

Oh, what a trifle from Mr. Mitterrand the great!
Oh, what a trite from you Mr. Ambassador!
For the one we're not ripe for democracy!
For the other our dream of freedom is an illusion!
Thank good heavens we are dreamers
And would retort: "ignorance and only ignorance
Would push any being to thinking
The thirst for freedom of any form
And anywhere in this world is an illusion!"

February, 8th 2004.

42

(41)

All amazement and confusion
And Man rules this world? Diversion!
Would one were god
Would have brought
Sunlight in the heart of the night
For all to see Man's little might
The world is Woman
And she at the command
Not Man!

(42)

In life all is driven to succeed
In life all is full
Of wilful
Intentions of forgetting
Procreation's generosity
Accounting for the great
Regret
Crowning deathbeds
With only reveries and no turning back !

04/03/2004.

(43)

I know one thing
That for the world means nothing:
Those excellent
At the art of pen
Holding will always find a broken pen
At lent!
An award for a draft
To cross the sea without a raft

(44)

Capitalise on Peace in whatever you
                              Do
                    Consider right the timing
                      Of any happening
                  And see how much peace of mind
                        You shall find
                      And how much your fear
                      And grieves disappear
                  With no need for a protective spear !

(45)

Forgiveness should be the first sign
The first sign
   Of Nobility
         Dignity
And   Integrity;
And accepting to live in the forgiven
Wrong is none but a great fall,
Cowardice and Folly
At their utmost.

(46)

Staying upright
Inwardly and upright
In your dealings
With your surroundings
Would allow you to stand,
Stand up and freely
               Move   on
Should the whole wide world
Under your feet crumble.

(47)

Cherish and cherish delight
                    Delight
In seeing none suffer
No   matter
Their creed
And kind
Delight fills the soul full
In seeing all with joy full,
Happy and of bliss full!

(48)

When asked about material
And the immaterial,
With enchantment
The muse sang:
"Seek not the materials
The materials
Of this world
For we are
99.99% immaterial."

(49)

"Pain and suffering
Have their claws in the living:
The Rich as well as the Poor,
And I wonder if there is a way,
                    A way of escaping
This…!" echoed the hurt
And without thought
I did retort,
"A perfectly clean conscience alone can…!"

(50)

Question: Who fathers
              Pain and suffering?
Answer: They are born of our
              Ignorant perspective!
Question: And who murders
Them?
Answer: Our enlightened
Souls within, keen
And following the blissful
Light within!

(51)

"Feeling hurt when wronged is natural."
Holds the adage
To which saying I say: "No!"
Every wrong must be played
Down
In order to move on
For life is forever
Fun!
Let not any wrong kill the fun!

(52)

To kill the Quiet truth
Some revert to shouts,
Screams,
Blackmail
And blames
And others to muteness!
How it is impossible for
Any of these to right
A wrong !

(53)

The load,
The load on my shoulder
Is that of a name's
Attributes,
Viz.   Nobility,
        Dignity,
And   Integrity!
And one must have these
To happily and proudly pride himself as one!

(54)

As a kid, I thought masks were only worn by masquerades,
And/or idiots and cowards
That coloured my Cameroonian childhood,
Growing up, I read of clowns
And had them replace the childhood masquerades
And thought they best fitted them! No! Mistake!
The politicians they fit Best!
And like my childhood ones,
Politicians use these to coerce fellow human beings

(55)

Intelligence no doubt
Is the architect behind the universe
And when humans
Begin thinking they were more intelligent
Than Intelligence,
I see a reflection of the pool,
The pool of ignorance,
That in which they swim
Swimming to an end unforetold!

(56)

The cutting edge of a blade
I thought was the sharpest,
No! No!
The sharpest I found
On the thinness of the wall
Separating Love from
Its other side, a word
I would All from
Their lexicons banished to warrant a harmonious world!

(57)

Unlike Vegetable
Life's not Perishable
But if left unconsumed
Rots away
Like the wasted day
Of a man's youth!
And thinking it Perishable!
Sores the heart
And one wishes his forever lasted. Alas!

(58)

Lost in the reverie of physical wellness
With not even the slightest trace of fear
And forward marching towards the Great Lake
The Great Dark Lake of worldly hustle and bustle
And would all quested instead the Great Dark Lake
Of silent knowledge by the inner light lit
And enlivened by this magic music
The magic music of the silent inner voice
All need to have for choice!

12/02/2006

(59)

The moroseness of dryness
And the politics of empty selfishness
Must be goads,
Goading humans to desiring the winds
And the Clouds
That bring the cheerful rains
To flood the dry lands
And snatch away the cheerlessness;
Leaving behind gladness…!

19/02/2006

(60)

Inner, inner light
Through which I seek peace,
Harmony,
Laughter,
Knowledge and wisdom;
And inwardly looking,
Your flashes blind
Me to the outside world
With darkness brightly lit.

28/02/2006

(61)

Question: Face to face with the ignorant,
        What do you do?
Answer: Give 'em the help
        You would in seeing someone
        Nose diving accidentally
        Lifting your hands and head up
        And exclaiming "Oh my God!"
        Will only pave their way
            To descending the dark pit,
        The dark pit of a worldless world!

19/03/2006

(62)

Even if enchained with songs of Cultural uniqueness
'N pushed by the wind that will blow filth
To soil the sanity of Human Spirit
Be not tempted to go marching,
Marching in the dark pit of this worldless world
In which King & Queen Ignorance rain
And in their Divine Right sweeps
               Fancy
And Imagination to generate fear
Of Everything & Everyone foreign

(63)

Reckon life and death are neighbours within us
Like happiness and sadness in us do reside
And the choices we make set aside
That which we desire needs no fuss
The bright frown on the face
The cloudy joy of the heart
All lay on that path
And show up when we choose they surface
Surfacing from that endless depth of the human entrails

25/03/06

(64)

When I heard a woman
Shout, shouting at a man:
"There are men out there,
Men out there to love me
Men out there to cherish me
And those to treat me like a queen…
Bla…! Bla…! Bla…!"
Silently, I told myself:
"Not until they taste of the quinine
You are, you will never see how loved
'N cherished you are and have been by a King!"

25/03/06

(65)

By day or by night
Like a knight or a knave
Like a king or a slave
All might or might not have taken delight
Delight in this life whose uncertain
Start makes the fateful end certain,
Making them of the end so scared
Whereas it should be preferred
Preferred for its solace

02/04/06

(66)

With gusto from within devouring us
That worst form of consumption, Ignorance
Is the real enemy
To be fought by the world around me!
Stunned by his omnipresence, tongue
Tight, my dreams and hopes
Hoping for a peaceful world full of hopes
For the aged and the young
Should egg awakening and stimulate us

05/04/06

(67)

A child could not hold his breath
Upon learning about a young man's death
And asked why death chose him;
And the bereaved father hearing him
Did with a deep sigh followed by a smile
Sought consolation for this child
Saying: "the bell was a call to walk to Freedom!
Choosing him to walk to his own Kingdom
Where he'll with no toil peacefully reign!

06/04/2006

(68)

      In the shallow grave,
What else could be seen but Ignorance
With its peculiar stance
To reaching heaven as a brave
And in such a dramatic struggle
With a life-long display of the puzzleless puzzle
Of the one and only way to heaven
With no knowledge of the Great Prussian
              Who saw all taking their own way to Heaven?

(69)

Doing their utmost, with their peculiar bent
As though Godsend
When everything seems to fade,
Fading out, poets live in the shade
To comfort the travelling cheerless
And in the twilight of this feeling
They quickly escape into it, meeting
With the terrible situation of these cheerless,
Striving that affection gets a better outcome!

27/04/2006

(70)

Busy, busy, busy,
Everyone is busy
With many bossy-busy with their vision,

Their impaired vision of the way to salvation
In whose name many a man met with doom
When as a child, yester night I dreamt of a boom!
Now I quest what colour riveting this stance
Would to the circumstance
Of mankind make bloom: blue, red, purple, yellow, pink,
green or brown...

23/09/2006

(71)

We have fought Wars!
We have won Wars!
We have Lost Wars!
Fought, won, and Lost All Wars
That brought none but Misery
Yet we failed to learn from their History
Telling their drive is much less the accumulation &
possession of weapon
And much more the use of the Tongue….
And the infant in me, gifted with reason quest
Why we let her loose…!

(72)

After celebrating their great achievement
Ignoring the definite end of men
These or those doctors
In their dying beds surrounded by doctors
Are helpless just when their pay
For living this life comes that day
They and their friends sort to employ arms,
The avail of which
Will never grant their wish
Live another day ! An extra day…!

26/09/2006

(73)

Which of Ignorance
And arrogance
Drives man to projecting himself
Over and above an elf
When pain and suffering
Do set their foot in
Leaving him in   this stress
To turn against his fellowman
To show he was more than man?

(74)

The crescent of this phase announces
A silent brightness
And anticipates joys of the calmness
As the full phase does the rowdy darkness
With the sadness of its dreariness
A spell casts on the psyche wards
Abandoning poets searching for words
And yearning the moonlight for their play
And bidding the bright silent sickle to stay!

(75)

How else can we style backing off,
Running away from trouble,
Other than cowardice?
Far from cowardice,
It takes a lot of guts
To spot
Trouble and step out of her way;
Facing trouble and knowing her outcome
Is utmost ignorance of arrogance born,
Far from the blissful…!

21/02/07

(76)

Having queried the path to inner peace,
We need question that of anger & rage
Patent through their fumes
And all generated by ignorant arrogance
Tilting the balance between mind and soul,
Self and the cosmic self,
The Intellect and Emotion,
Consciousness and unconsciousness
All elements Peace Lovers must keep in check!

(77)

We need not fool ourselves;
Fooling ourselves with endless
Service attendance and prayers
To come by inner peace…!

How then can we know inner peace?

Come to terms with our inner beings!
Not making of violence a resort
To solving problems and making mountains
Out of mole hills:
Peace with ourselves, our surroundings and the Lord is the
Way!

(78)

A person can trick another
Tricking him into a relationship
And taking him far
Far, far away from all relatives
With dreams of keeping him submissive
But can't trick herself,
Tricking herself to loving
Even when the tricked is unfailing
In his unconditional love for the trickster…

(79)

Wisdom, Good sense
And Sensibility,
Ignorance
Or Arrogance
Might stand in stead
Of the justification
For some human action
But none would ever, ever
Do for violence resulting from anger !

28/03/07

(80)

Thinking of a possible platitude
I found one highest in altitude:
The possibility
Of a wise man triplicating
Three fools
And the total impossibility
For a trillion fools
Replicating

A wise man.

12/04/2007

(81)

Borne from within
And not from without,
Despondency dwells in
And never out !
And parents might hold the world to blame
And if not fooled by ignorance may look in,
Within their innerselves
And set all out and without
Free of blame

12/04/2007

(82)

Feeling pity
And not Love
For another human being
Is born of ignorance:
Fooling oneself of being
Better than a fellow
Traveller, one in this journey towards the grave
But loving the other for being human
Is born of the cognizance
Of the oneness of humanity

(83)

From under his sleeves
A local priest
Came up with a parable
And the unbelieving ears of a faithful
Made his mouth of question full
And he shouted out: "why not,
Why not, make of faith and not
The earthly church the cornerstone,
The cornerstone of belief
Even if all will rot like leaves?

(84)

When striving for things better
As would a dove,
Never choose money & power
                    Over
Love
          And   Peace
And voice nothing in anger
For that which is of anger
Born is always bitter.

21/05/2007

(85)

Let not looks pull
Away from faith, a faithful
For faith should be founded upon
That inner quest and find
And not the act of believing
Just that which has been told
By religions and priests
Making of martyrdom
The sole path to the heavenly kingdom.

(86)

Tossed left and right;
And left to reflect on man's plight:
   Economic, social, cultural
            Political and historical
               Narrow mindedness
I helplessly found wisdom and happiness
Stifled with the burial
Of criticism
Ignoring it the apogee of patriotism…!

22/05/2007

(87)

A world with discrimination
And hate plagued? Wondered
The cheerful baby
       That accompanies Man at birth! Burning with the
            desire for poetry
       To portray its inner cheerfulness
This baby embarked on exploring
The depths of human psyche, questing
Why over the ages poets have traded words for feelings:
To illuminate their own experiences…?
       To better the perception of what
          Humans really are?

(88)

Out and about
And in my mind no doubt
I know a fact:
Poets & only poets will kill death in fact
For only these word warriors
Can beat and smelt their pens,
Beat & smelt their pens into guns,
Bullets, swords, spears and spades
With which to kill and inter death;
And drumsticks with which to drum a dirge
As they take death to the grave!

(89)

Seeing people die
A child watched others cry
And for many a man like dirt
Treated, he with them mourns the dead
                    Not those at the helm
                    Who stole the emblem
                    And piece of pie
He'd stood for his wishful thinking
                                    Of reviving

Deeds from the Heart done!

01/08/2007

(90)

Some lives are riddled with riddles
And others plagued with needles
Yet mine is the riddle itself
With poetry some lives are embellished
And mine is the poem itself
While others' lives are by broken dreams   tarnished,
I strive to make mine wholesome whole
And with finesse my whole
Life I will live it wholly
                    Ho(l)ly.

(91)

Cherish many things in life
Wish for many things in life
Ignore neither Godliness
Nor the humanness
Of humankind and let not the latter
Dampen your quest for the former
Enthusiasm in Godliness is divine
Only if it doesn't affect one like wine
Blinding him to the realities of our humanness

06/11/2007

(92)

Waves! Waves! Waves!
I don't know, I don't know, I don't know
Ha! ha! ha! Ha! ha! ha!
Aye! Aye! Aye!
Yah! Yah! Yah!
No! no! no!
Want to know, want to know, want to know
Yes! Yes! Yes!
I think I see! I see! I see!
Not the sea! Not the sea!
Not the sea…! I see

12/11/2007

(93)

Caring for things
Heavenly
Never made one a better man
And caring less for things
Earthly
Should not make one a lesser man
Caring neither way takes one to the centre
And not to the edges;
The birthplace of ladenism for ages.

(94)

Wondering why species do not appellation change
As would humans when they location change
A dragonfly on a rose perching
Watched in disbelief our creed fighting
Fighting because one from another part of this world
Came and the other in this would a word
Or words coin for the appellation of the former
Fugees, ignorant migrants and the hyphenated name-game
And with ignorance would this class shouldered the blame

(95)

The beauty of roses,
The beauty of roses,
Is that they never go by the names:
African, European, Asian, American, nor do they identify
with such accolades as Cameroonian, Dutch, French, English,
or German.
In line with the language of emotions
They are not in terms of origin expressed
Yet, the sausage making side of humans
Stands between the one world and one mankind

(96)

Floral leaves and petals
Make the flower
And so do Black, White and yellow
Mankind make!
With the fighting in today's world
One between the I... bomb developer
And the Western Supremacy defender
Would yellow's Artistic withdrawal
On the phases of the moon and the sun reflecting
In Black and White instil some thinking.

(97)

What will ignorance not make us see?
Queried the blind upon hearing
People say: "The blind we should pity,
For they're sightless!"
And the blind exclaimed
"Ignorance makes us see a treeless
Forest full of emptiness.
'Coz our blindness gives us sight,
A sight in mind brighter than light

(98)

Give me no nonsense!
Give me no good sense!
Give me any other reason
And I will tell you it is unreason
For a teacher to spur mercifully
And not mercilessly
To goad on that inborn reaction
To ceaselessly thirst for knowledge
In pupils, even in those who know no college.

(99)

Born human,
Live human,
Act human
And play neither God
Nor the devil and his advocate
Thinking it makes you great
Only to open the door for Ignorance
To come nibble the potentials
Of your humanness.

(100)

Out of the haze I remember a dream
With children as were never before seen
And to the tune of supreme verses,
Super colourful than dresses
Ever man did see,
Dancing as they ushered Ignorance into the sea
And none of the lines recalled perchance,
The joy of their dance
Forever dwells with this solitary dreamer.

Wishful thinking

Would all were
Only in complexion dark
Or Black
Not having
Any imagining
Of such a complexion…
How peaceful
Our world would be
      And we as merry as would be a bee!

Epilogue to Epigrams

These doggerels
Might have made you laugh
Might have made you cry
And much less, think for those who think
Laugh, cry and think
Might be far removed from traditional literature
But, to this persona, they constitute
The path,
The path to the shore of inner quiet
Warranting sail like the cool calm breeze of a waveless sea
That
Many in our busy world only come by in their cavern!

Epilogue to the Prologue

Seeing a bright blue sky
Its haziness
Clouding the earth
And the vegetation screening the clouds
For all to see true
Blue
And breathe fresh air pure
On earth
All sum Epigrams' mirth.